# THE Movie Songs BIG BOOK

Alfred Publishing Co., Inc.
16320 Roscoe Blvd., Suite 100
P.O. Box 10003
Van Nuys, CA 91410-0003
alfred.com

ISBN-10: 0-7390-4575-X
ISBN-13: 978-0-7390-4575-6

# CONTENTS

| TITLE | MOVIE | PAGE |
|-------|-------|------|
| Adelieland | Happy Feet | 3 |
| And All That Jazz | Chicago | 6 |
| Aquarius | Hair | 18 |
| Arthur's Theme (Best That You Can Do) | Arthur | 14 |
| Beautiful Stranger | Austin Powers: The Spy Who Shagged Me | 21 |
| Beauty and the Beast | Beauty and the Beast | 32 |
| Believe | The Polar Express | 28 |
| Billy's Theme | The Departed | 37 |
| Can You Read My Mind? | Superman | 44 |
| Can't Fight the Moonlight | Coyote Ugly | 47 |
| Charade | Charade | 52 |
| The Circle of Life | The Lion King | 56 |
| Corynorhinus (Surveying the Ruins) | Batman Begins | 61 |
| Crazy 'Bout My Baby | Meet the Fockers | 64 |
| The Departed Tango | The Departed | 71 |
| Doctor Dolittle | Doctor Dolittle | 74 |
| Double Trouble | Harry Potter and the Prisoner of Azkaban | 80 |
| Evergreen | A Star Is Born | 90 |
| Everything Burns | Fantastic Four | 96 |
| Eye of the Tiger | Rocky III | 85 |
| Fawkes the Phoenix | Harry Potter and the Chamber of Secrets | 104 |
| Flashdance...What a Feeling | Flashdance | 108 |
| Gonna Fly Now | Rocky | 118 |
| Hedwig's Theme | Harry Potter and the Sorcerer's Stone | 113 |
| Hero | Spider-Man | 122 |
| Hogwarts' Hymn | Harry Potter and the Goblet of Fire™ | 128 |
| Hopelessly Devoted to You | Grease | 134 |
| In Dreams (featured in "The Breaking of the Fellowship") | Lord of the Rings: The Fellowship of the Ring | 131 |
| James Bond Theme (Bond vs. Oakenfold) | Die Another Day | 138 |
| Lady in the Water (End Titles) | Lady in the Water | 148 |
| Live and Let Die | Live and Let Die | 150 |
| Mystic River Theme | Mystic River | 154 |
| Night Fever | Saturday Night Fever | 143 |
| The Notebook (Main Title) | The Notebook | 156 |
| Over the Rainbow | The Wizard of Oz | 162 |
| Parade of Ants | The Ant Bully | 166 |
| The Pink Panther | The Pink Panther | 168 |
| Platoon Swims | Flags of Our Fathers | 170 |
| The Poseidon | Poseidon | 159 |
| Raiders March | Raiders of the Lost Ark | 172 |
| Raindrops Keep Falling on My Head | Butch Cassidy and the Sundance Kid | 176 |
| The Rose | The Rose | 180 |
| Singin' in the Rain | Singin' in the Rain | 184 |
| Somewhere, My Love (Lara's Theme) | Dr. Zhivago | 188 |
| Song from M*A*S*H (Suicide Is Painless) | M*A*S*H | 191 |
| A Spoonful of Sugar | Mary Poppins | 194 |
| Star Wars (Main Title) | Star Wars®: Episode III, Revenge of the Sith | 200 |
| Streets of Philadelphia | Philadelphia | 197 |
| Theme from A Summer Place | A Summer Place | 217 |
| Superman Returns (Suite) | Superman Returns | 204 |
| Syriana Theme | Syriana | 211 |
| That's What Friends Are For | Night Shift | 214 |
| Under the Sea | The Little Mermaid | 220 |
| Up Where We Belong | An Officer and a Gentleman | 230 |
| Victor's Piano Solo | Corpse Bride | 234 |
| Way Back Into Love | Music and Lyrics | 236 |
| Who's That Girl? | Who's That Girl | 243 |
| A Window to the Past | Harry Potter and the Prisoner of Azkaban | 254 |
| Wonka's Welcome Song | Charlie and the Chocolate Factory | 248 |
| The Work Song | Cinderella | 252 |

# ADELIELAND
(from HAPPY FEET)

Composed by
JOHN POWELL

Moderately bright latin ♩ = 132

Adelieland - 3 - 1

# AND ALL THAT JAZZ

Words by
FRED EBB

Music by
JOHN KANDER

Moderately slow, deliberately

12

And All That Jazz - 8 - 7

*From "ARTHUR" an ORION PICTURES release through WARNER BROS.*

# ARTHUR'S THEME
## (Best That You Can Do)

Words and Music by
BURT BACHARACH, CAROL BAYER SAGER,
CHRISTOPHER CROSS and PETER ALLEN

Once in your life, you'll find
Ar- thur, he does what he

# AQUARIUS

Words by
JAMES RADO and GEROME RAGNI

Music by
GALT MacDERMOT

Aquarius - 3 - 1

*From the Motion Picture AUSTIN POWERS: The Spy Who Shagged Me*

# BEAUTIFUL STRANGER

Words and Music by
MADONNA CICCONE and WILLIAM ORBIT

Beautiful Stranger - 7 - 1

22

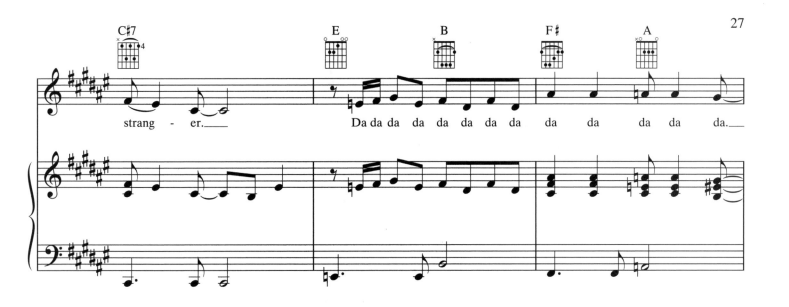

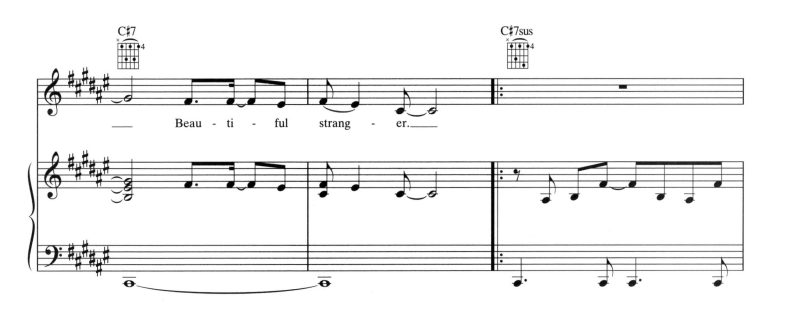

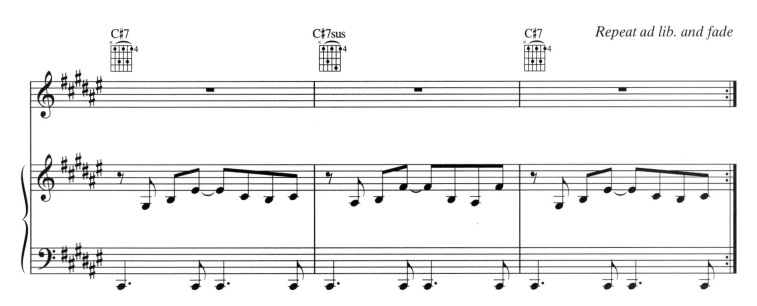

From THE POLAR EXPRESS
# BELIEVE

Words and Music by
GLEN BALLARD and ALAN SILVESTRI

Moderately slow ♩ = 80

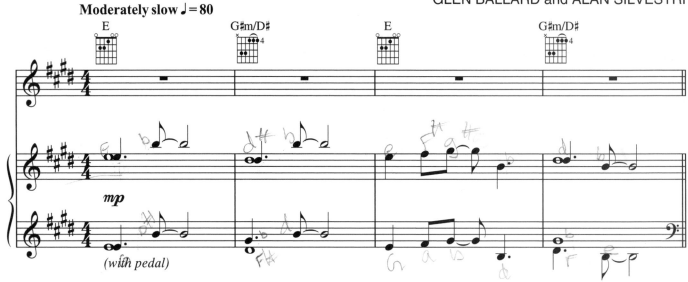

*(with pedal)*

Verse:

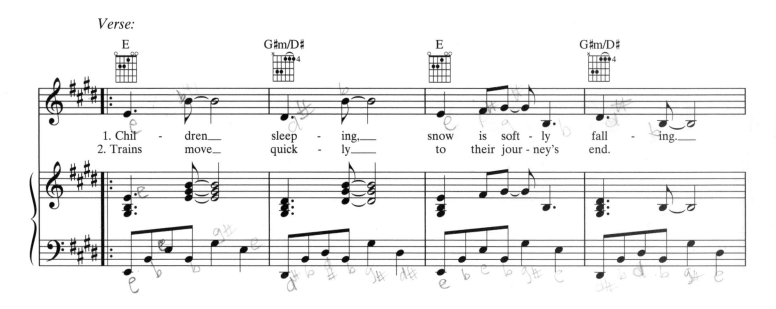

1. Chil - dren___ sleep - ing, snow is soft - ly fall - ing.___
2. Trains move___ quick - ly___ to their jour - ney's end.

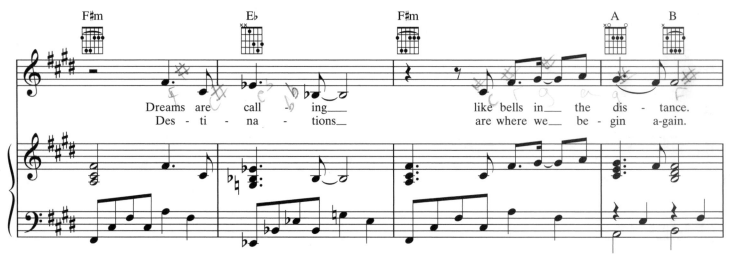

Dreams are call - ing___ like bells in___ the dis - tance.
Des - ti - na - tions___ are where we___ be - gin a - gain.

Believe - 4 - 1

Believe - 4 - 4

*(from Walt Disney's "Beauty and the Beast")*

# BEAUTY AND THE BEAST

Words by
HOWARD ASHMAN

Music by
ALAN MENKEN

# BILLY'S THEME
## (from THE DEPARTED)

Composed by
HOWARD SHORE

**Moderately slow** ♩ = 80

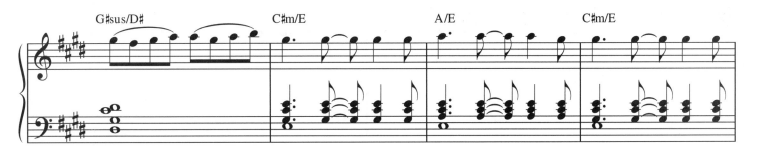

Billy's Theme - 7 - 1

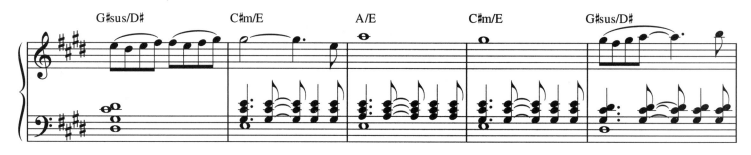

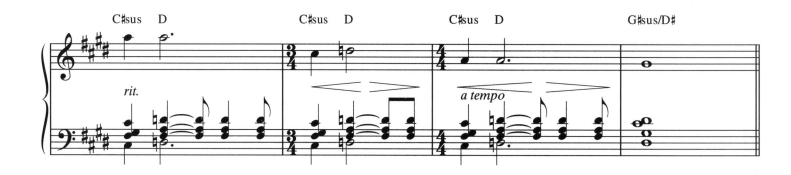

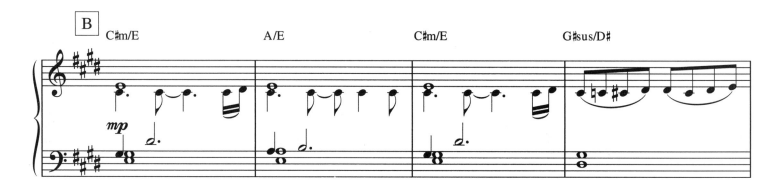

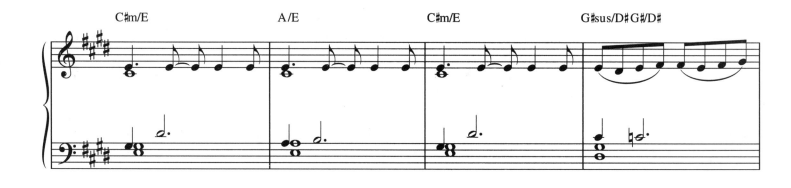

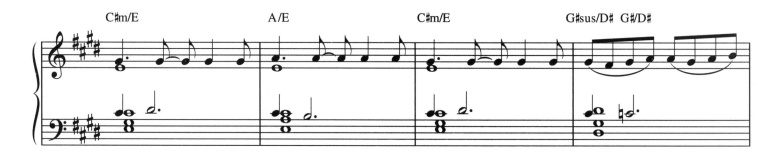

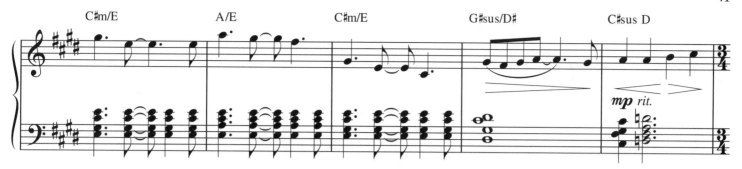

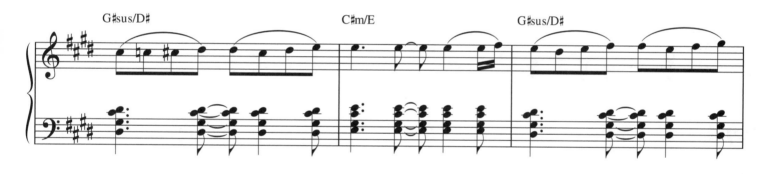

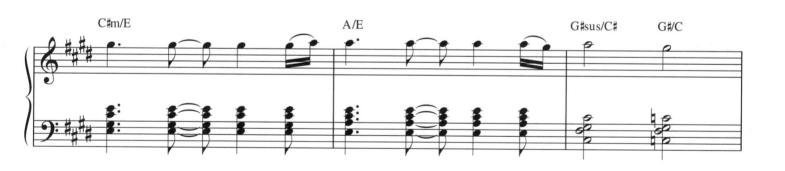

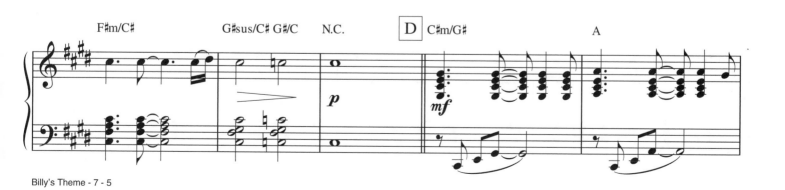

42

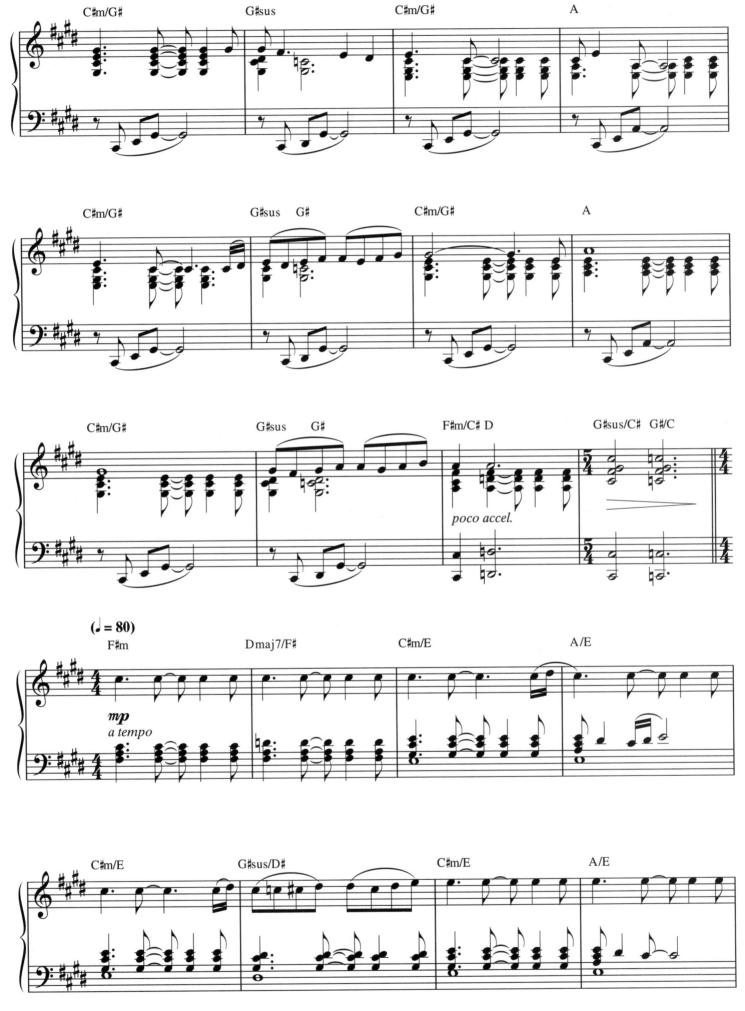

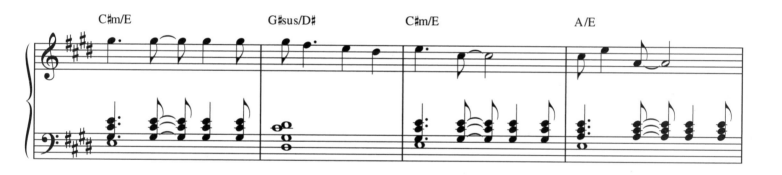

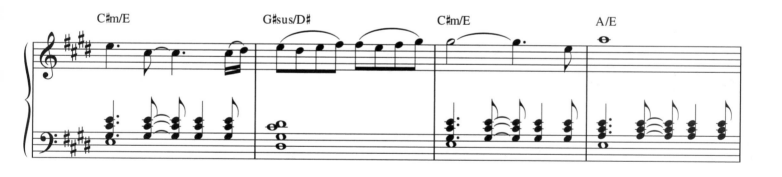

*Love Theme from "SUPERMAN" A Warner Bros. Picture*

# CAN YOU READ MY MIND?

Lyric by
**LESLIE BRICUSSE**

Music by
**JOHN WILLIAMS**

46

Can You Read My Mind? - 3 - 3

# CAN'T FIGHT THE MOONLIGHT

(Theme from Coyote Ugly)

Words and Music by
DIANE WARREN

Can't Fight the Moonlight - 5 - 1

# CHARADE

Words by
JOHNNY MERCER

Music by
HENRY MANCINI

Charade - 4 - 1

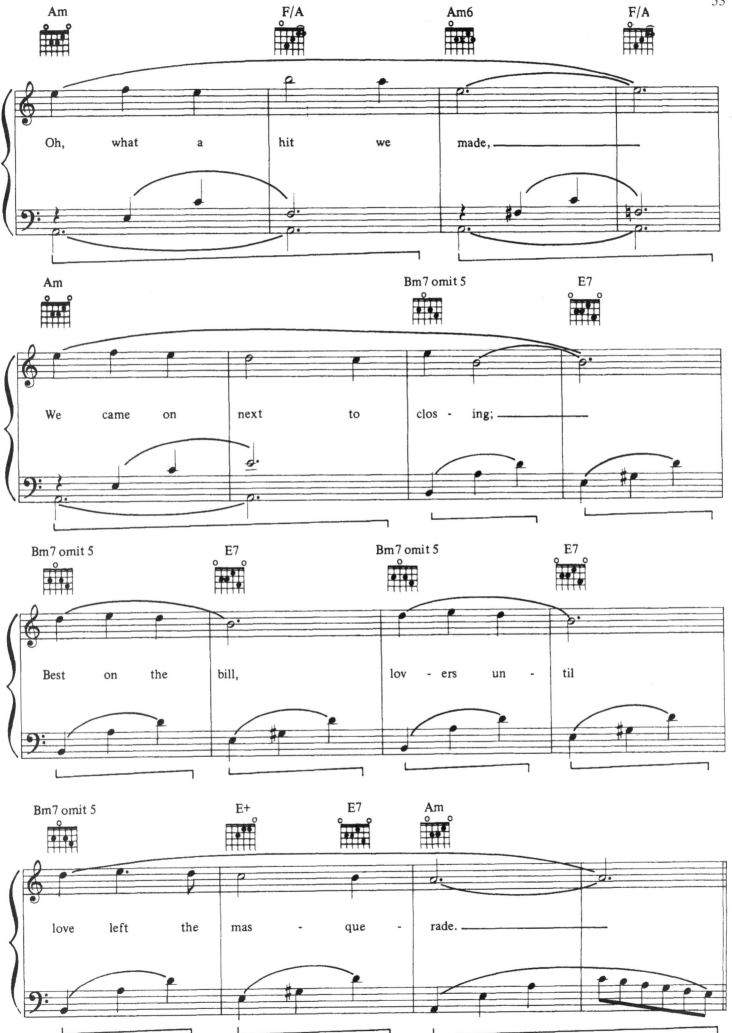

*(from Walt Disney's "The Lion King")*

# THE CIRCLE OF LIFE

Lyrics by
TIM RICE

Music by
ELTON JOHN

The Circle of Life - 5 - 1

58

60

from *BATMAN BEGINS*

# CORYNORHINUS
## (Surveying the Ruins)

Composed by HANS FLORIAN ZIMMER,
JAMES NEWTON HOWARD, MELVYN THOMAS WESSON,
RAMIN DJAWADI and LORNE DAVID RODERICK BALFE

**Moderately slow, rubato (♩ = 72)**

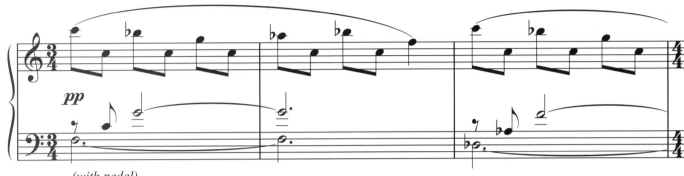

*(with pedal)*

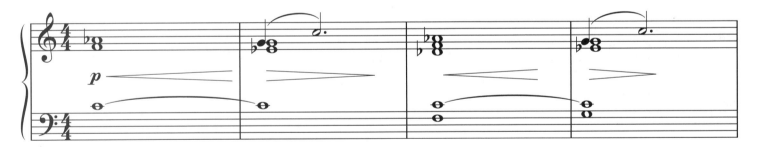

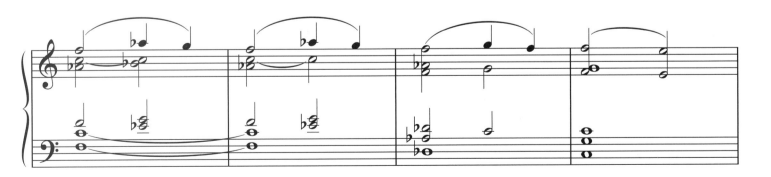

Corynorhinus (Surveying the Ruins) - 3 - 1

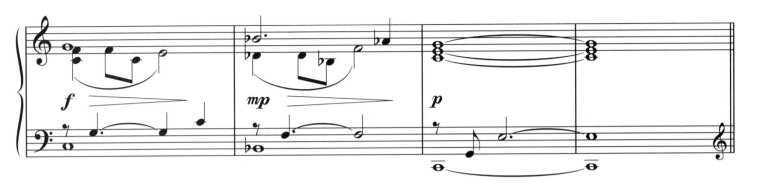

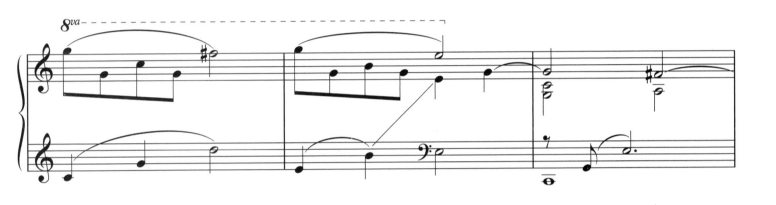

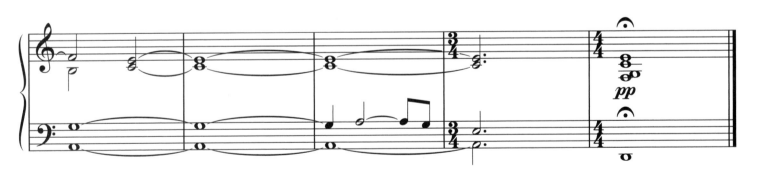

# CRAZY 'BOUT MY BABY
## (from the motion picture *Meet the Fockers*)

Words and Music by
RANDY NEWMAN

70

zy 'bout my ba - by, cra - zy 'bout my ba - by.

Cra - zy 'bout my ba-by; my ba-by's cra - zy 'bout me.

I'm cra - zy 'bout my ba-by; my ba-by's cra - zy 'bout me.

ad lib. fills

Crazy 'Bout My Baby - 7 - 7

# THE DEPARTED TANGO

Composed by
HOWARD SHORE

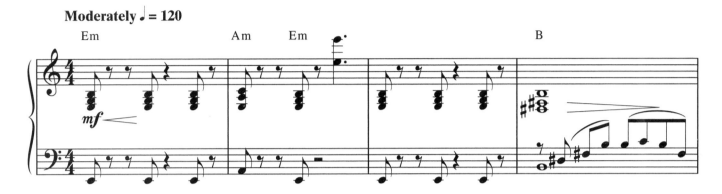

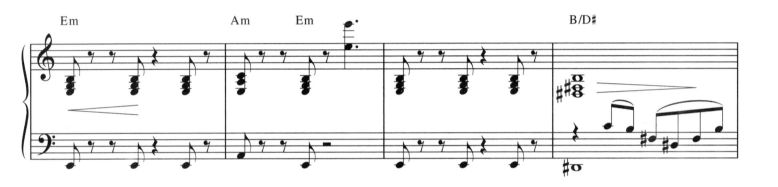

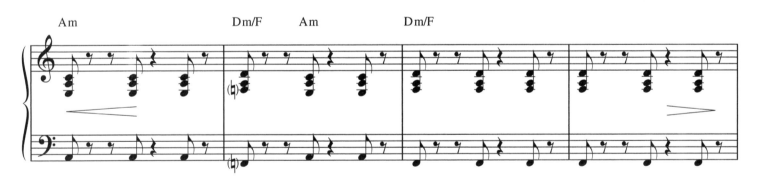

The Departed Tango - 3 - 1

72

# DOCTOR DOLITTLE

Words and Music by
LESLIE BRICUSSE

Doctor Dolittle - 6 - 1

78

Doctor Dolittle - 6 - 5

From Warner Bros. Pictures' HARRY POTTER AND THE PRISONER OF AZKABAN

# DOUBLE TROUBLE

Music by
**JOHN WILLIAMS**

**Medieval in spirit (♩ = 92)**

**Spiritedly**

Dou - ble, dou - ble toil and trou - ble; fire_____ burn and caul - dron bub - ble.

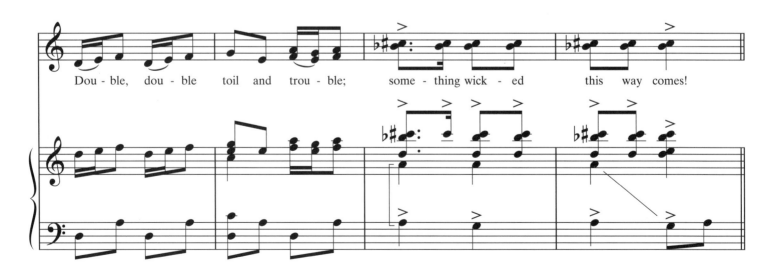

Dou - ble, dou - ble toil and trou - ble; some - thing wick - ed this way comes!

Double Trouble - 5 - 1

**Driving now, with a "swagger"**

84

# EYE OF THE TIGER
## (THEME FROM ROCKY III)

Words and Music by
FRANKIE SULLIVAN III and JIM PETERIK

Eye of the Tiger - 5 - 1

86

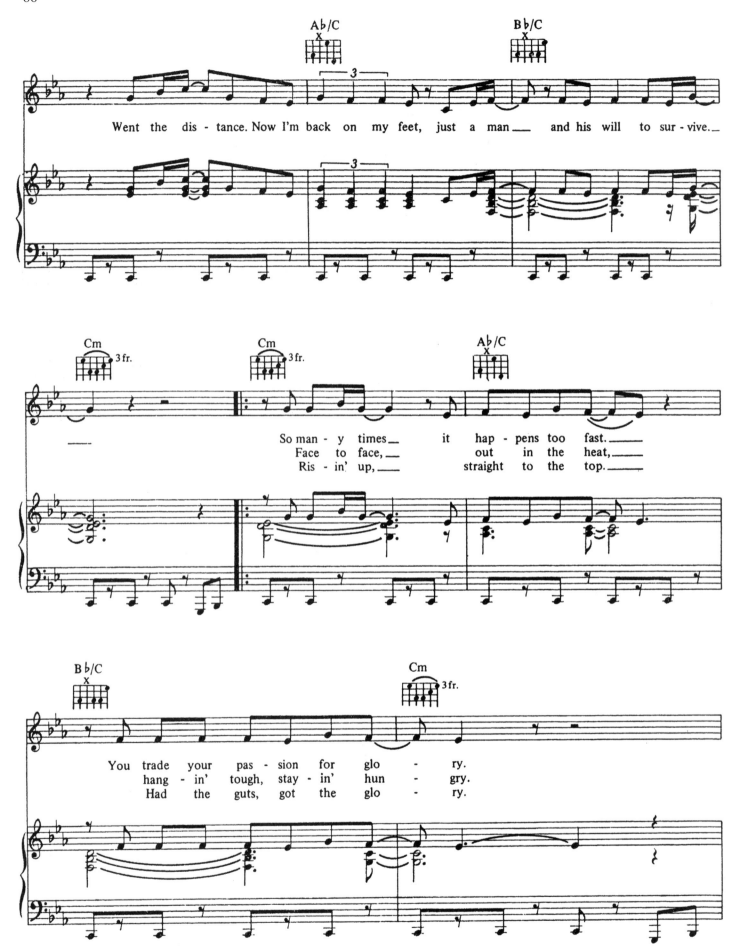

Eye of the Tiger - 5 - 2

# EVERGREEN
(Love Theme from "A STAR IS BORN")

Words by
PAUL WILLIAMS

Music by
BARBRA STREISAND

Evergreen - 6 - 1

93

Evergreen - 6 - 4

94

*From the Wind-up Records release "Fantastic 4: The Album"*

# EVERYTHING BURNS

Words and Music by
BEN MOODY

*All vocals written at pitch.

Everything Burns - 8 - 1

Bm(4)    A(9)

wrapped in all of the prom - is - es_____ that

Bm(4)/F♯    Gmaj13

no_____ one seems_____ to_____ keep._____

Bm(4)    A(9)

She no long - er cries_____ to her - self,_____ no

Bm(4)/F♯    Gmaj13

tears_____ left to wash a - way._____

98

*Verse 2:*

2. Walk - ing___ through life un - no - ticed,

know - ing___ that no one___ cares.___

Too con - sumed___ in their mas - que - rade,___

*Chorus:*

*From Warner Bros. Pictures' HARRY POTTER AND THE CHAMBER OF SECRETS*

# FAWKES THE PHOENIX

Music by
**JOHN WILLIAMS**

Fawkes the Phoenix - 4 - 1

106

# FLASHDANCE... WHAT A FEELING

Words by
**KEITH FORSEY and IRENE CARA**

Music by
**GIORGIO MORODER**

Steadily

110

now_____

(life)_____

What a feel - ing._____

*From Warner Bros. Pictures' HARRY POTTER AND THE SORCERER'S STONE*

# HEDWIG'S THEME

Music by
**JOHN WILLIAMS**

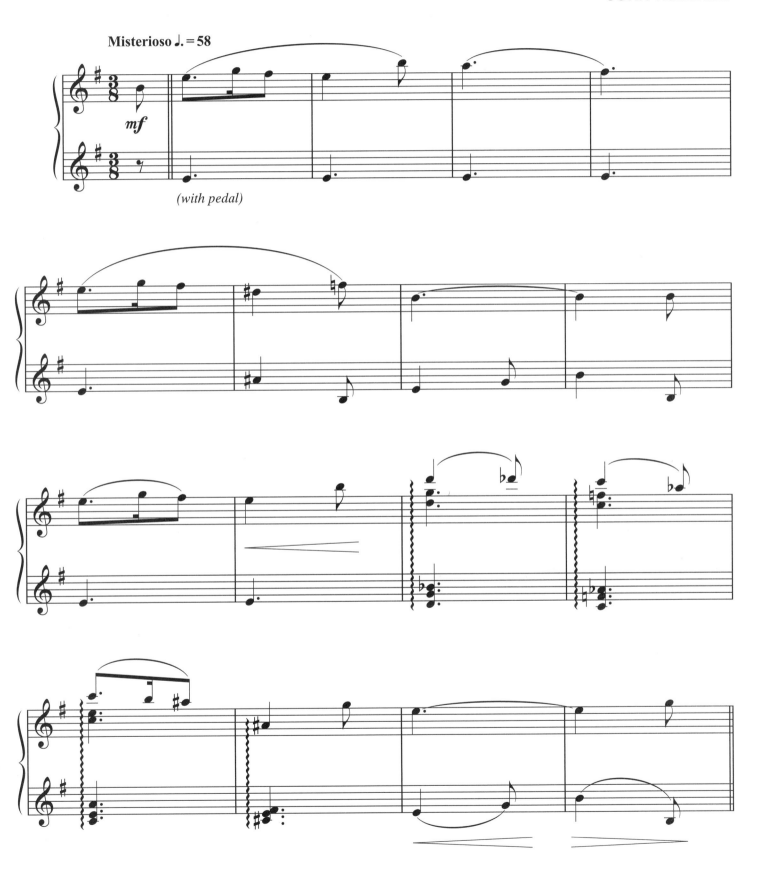

Hedwig's Theme - 5 - 1

Hedwig's Theme - 5 - 3

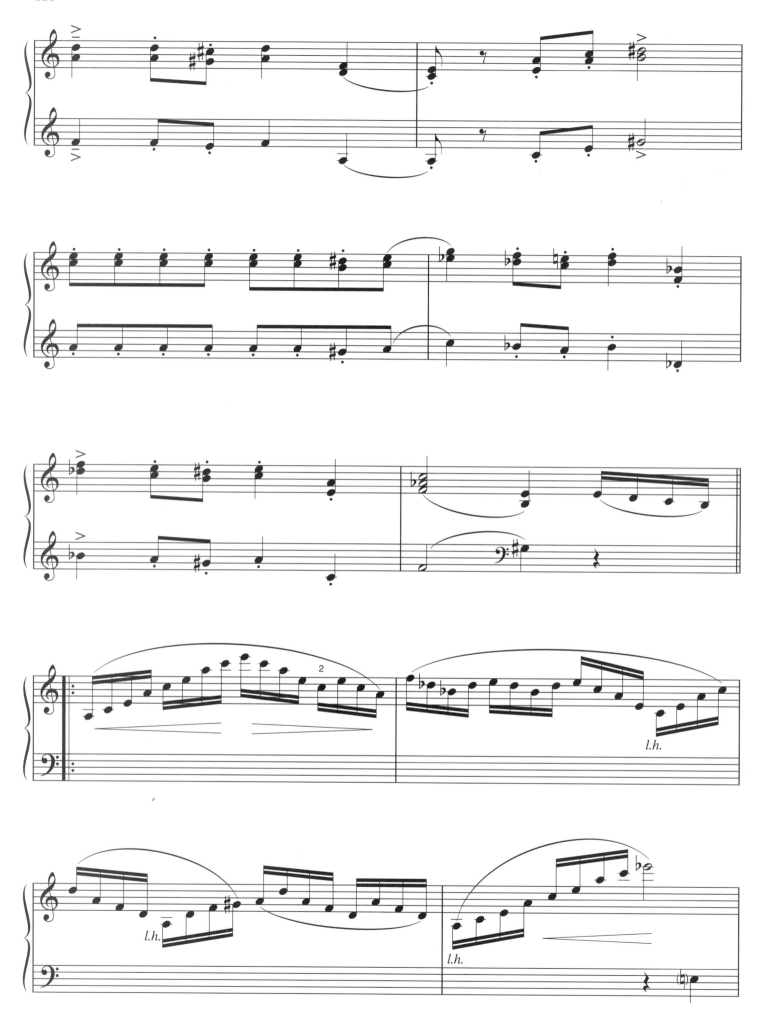

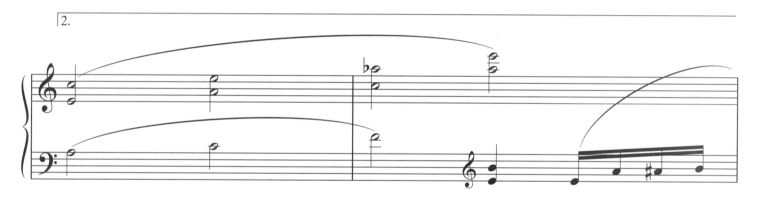

# (Theme from "Rocky")
# GONNA FLY NOW

Words and Music by
BILL CONTI, AYN ROBBINS
and CAROL CONNORS

120

Gonna Fly Now - 4 - 3

*From the Columbia Pictures Motion Picture SPIDER-MAN*

# HERO

Words and Music by
CHAD KROEGER

Slowly ♩. = 48

*Verse 1:*

1. I am so___ high,___ I can hear___ heav - en._____

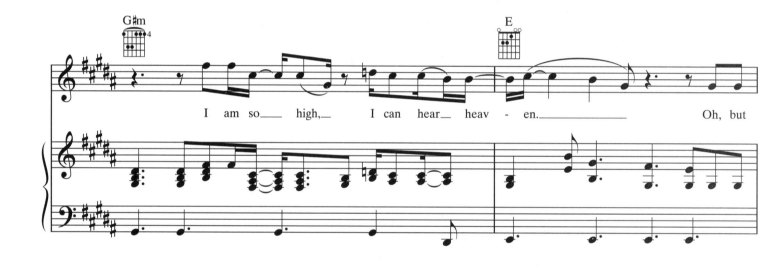

I am so___ high,___ I can hear___ heav - en._____ Oh, but

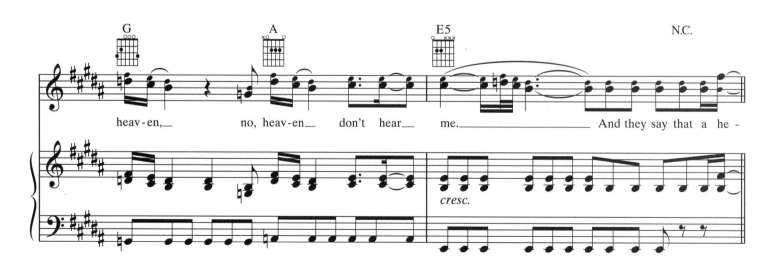

heav-en,___ no, heav-en___ don't hear___ me._____ And they say that a he-

Hero - 6 - 1

124

Hero - 6 - 3

126

# HOGWARTS' HYMN

By PATRICK DOYLE

**Nobilmente con expressivo** (♩ = 69)

Hogwarts' Hymn - 3 - 1

# IN DREAMS
## (featured in "The Breaking Of The Fellowship")

Words and Music by
FRAN WALSH and
HOWARD SHORE

# HOPELESSLY DEVOTED TO YOU

Words and Music by
JOHN FARRAR

Hopelessly Devoted to You - 4 - 1

Hopelessly Devoted to You - 4 - 2

136

137

Hopelessly Devoted to You - 4 - 4

# JAMES BOND THEME

(Bond vs. Oakenfold)

Music by MONTY NORMAN
Remix by PAUL OAKENFOLD

James Bond Theme - 5 - 1

*With a slight swing feel*

*To Coda* ⊕

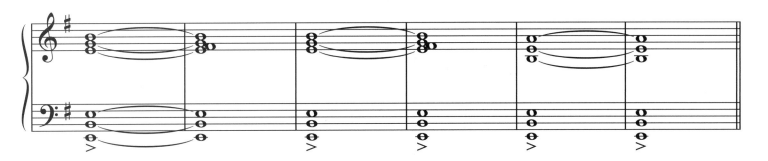

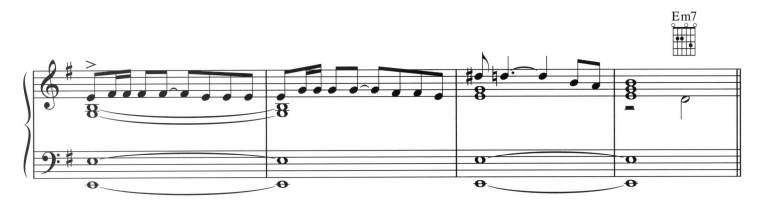

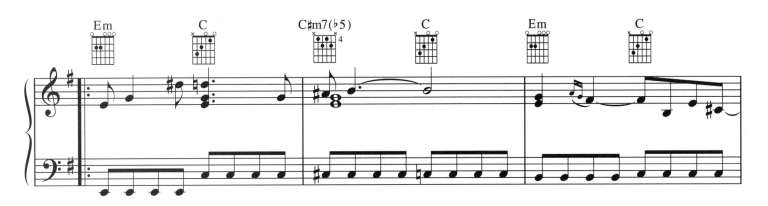

James Bond Theme - 5 - 4

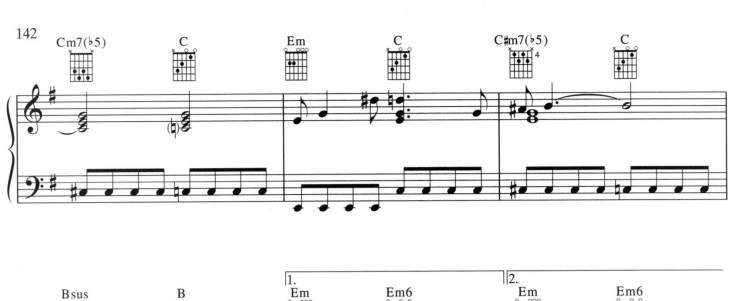

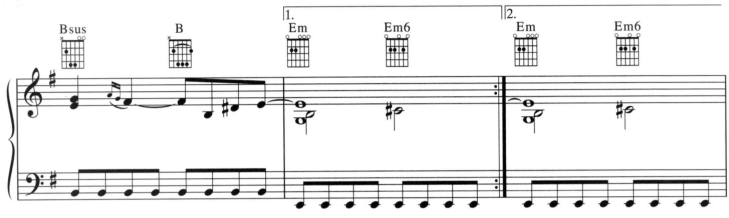

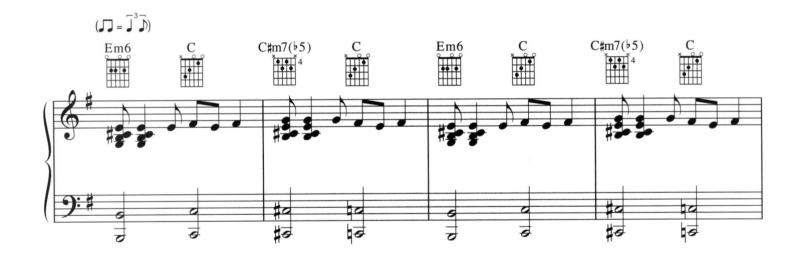

# NIGHT FEVER

Words and Music by
BARRY GIBB, MAURICE GIBB
and ROBIN GIBB

Night Fever - 5 - 1

145

Night Fever - 5 - 3

146

Night Fever - 5 - 4

# LADY IN THE WATER
# (END TITLES)

By JAMES NEWTON HOWARD

**Slowly, with expression (♩ = 56)**

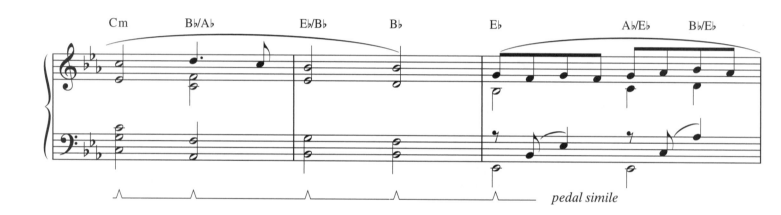

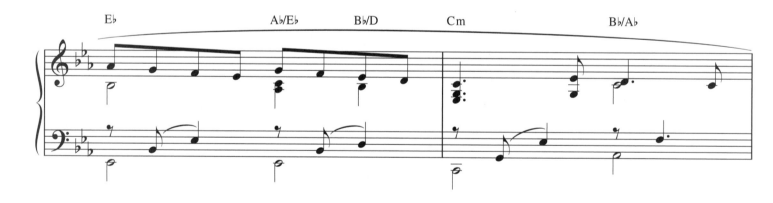

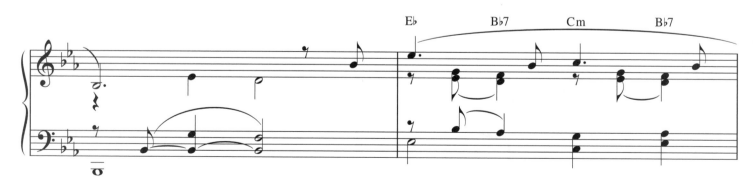

Lady in the Water - 2 - 1

*From the United Artists Motion Picture "LIVE AND LET DIE"*

# LIVE AND LET DIE

Words and Music by
PAUL McCARTNEY and LINDA McCARTNEY

Live and Let Die - 4 - 1

152

Live and Let Die - 4 - 3

give the oth - er fel - low hell!_____

*D.C. al Coda*

*Coda*

# MYSTIC RIVER THEME

By
CLINT EASTWOOD

Mystic River Theme - 2 - 1

# THE NOTEBOOK
## (Main Title)

Written by
AARON ZIGMAN

**Slowly, with expression** (♩=58)

*Più mosso*

**A little faster** (♩=69)

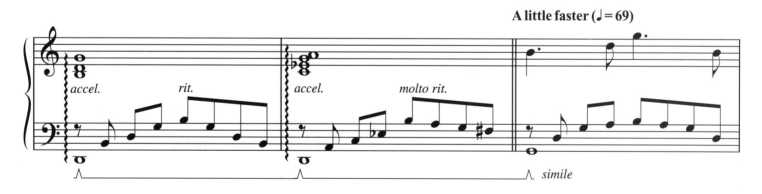

The Notebook - 3 - 1

158

The Notebook - 3 - 3

# THE POSEIDON

By
KLAUS BADELT

160

*Featured in the MGM Picture "THE WIZARD OF OZ"*

# OVER THE RAINBOW

Lyric by
E.Y. HARBURG

Music by
HAROLD ARLEN

When all the world is a hope-less jum-ble and the rain-drops tum-ble all a-round,

heav - en o-pens a mag-ic lane.

When all the clouds dark-en up the sky-way, there's a rain-bow high-way to be found,

Over the Rainbow - 4 - 1

# PARADE OF ANTS

## From "The Ant Bully"

By JOHN DEBNEY

**Moderately, with a heavy jungle beat** ♩ = 112

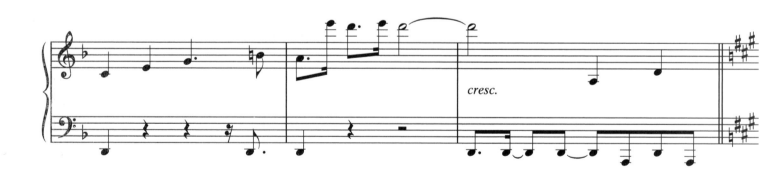

Parade of Ants - 2 - 1

*Theme Song from the Mirisch-G&E Production, "THE PINK PANTHER," a United Artists Release*

# THE PINK PANTHER

Music by
HENRY MANCINI

Moderately Mysterioso

The Pink Panther - 2 - 2

# PLATOON SWIMS
### (from FLAGS OF OUR FATHERS)

Composed by
CLINT EASTWOOD

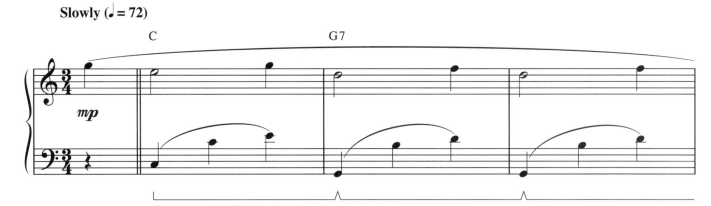

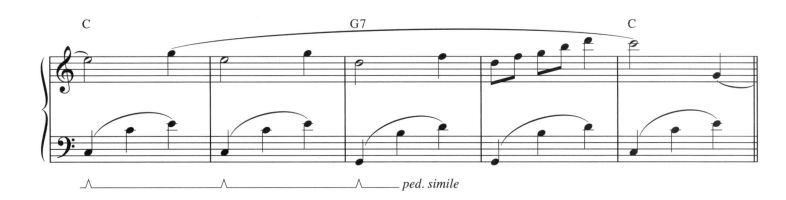

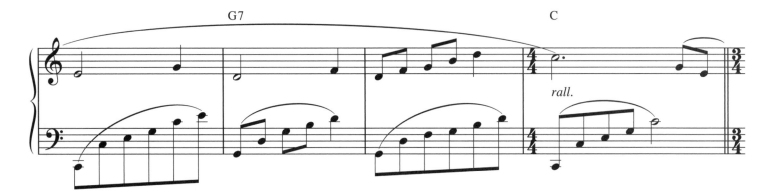

Platoon Swims - 2 - 1

# RAIDERS MARCH
## (From "Raiders of the Lost Ark")

By
**JOHN WILLIAMS**

Raiders March - 4 - 1

*simile*

Raiders March - 4 - 4

# RAINDROPS KEEP FALLIN' ON MY HEAD

Words by
HAL DAVID

Music by
BURT BACHARACH

Raindrops Keep Fallin' on My Head - 4 - 1

178

soon be turn - in' red.        Cry - in's not for me        'cause

I'm nev - er gon - na stop the rain        by com-plain-in'.        Be - cause I'm

free        noth - in's wor - ry - in'        me._____

*From the Twentieth Century-Fox Motion Picture "THE ROSE"*

# THE ROSE

Words and Music by
AMANDA McBROOM

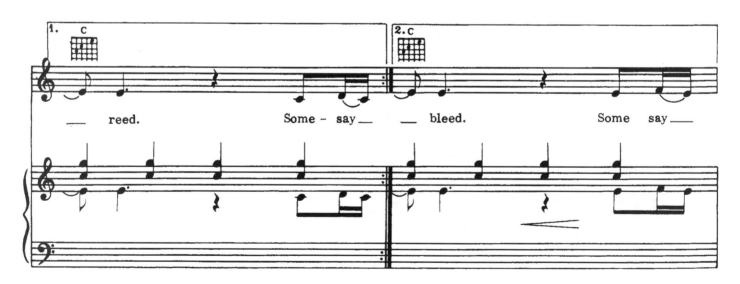

The Rose - 4 - 1

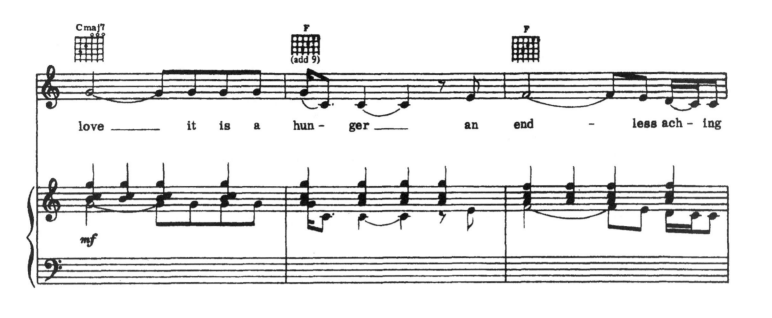

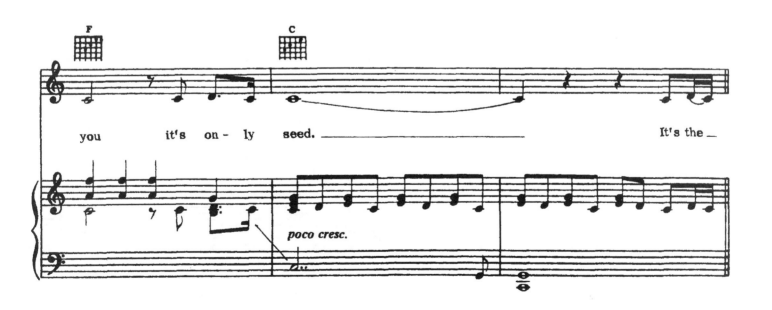

# SINGIN' IN THE RAIN

Lyric by
ARTHUR FREED

Music by
NACIO HERB BROWN

Singin' in the Rain - 4 - 1

186

*To Coda*

Singin' in the Rain - 4 - 3

*METRO-GOLDWYN-MAYER presents DAVID LEAN'S FILM "DOCTOR ZHIVAGO"*

# SOMEWHERE, MY LOVE
## (Lara's Theme From "Doctor Zhivago")

Lyric by
PAUL FRANCIS WEBSTER

Music by
MAURICE JARRE

190

Somewhere, My Love - 3 - 3

# SONG FROM M*A*S*H

*(Suicide Is Painless)*

Lyric by MIKE ALTMAN

Music by JOHNNY MANDEL

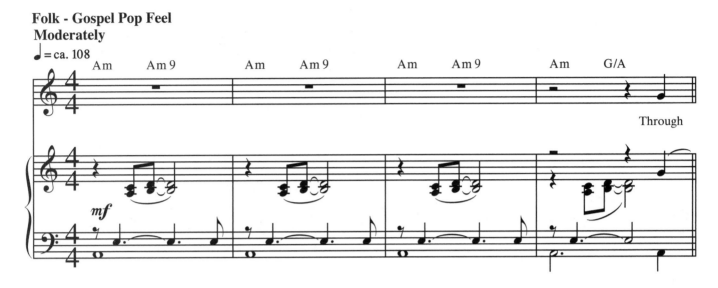

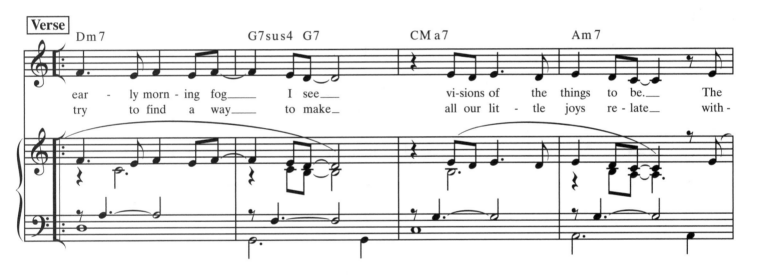

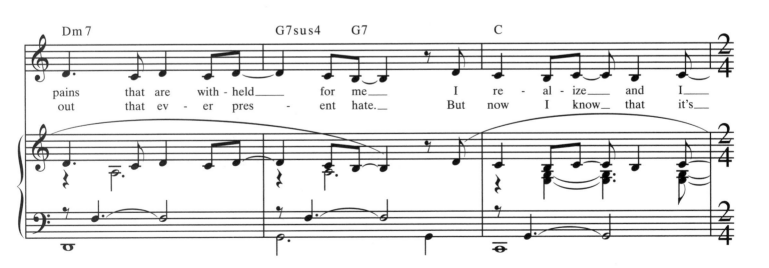

Song from M*A*S*H - 3 - 1

**Rubato - Slowly**

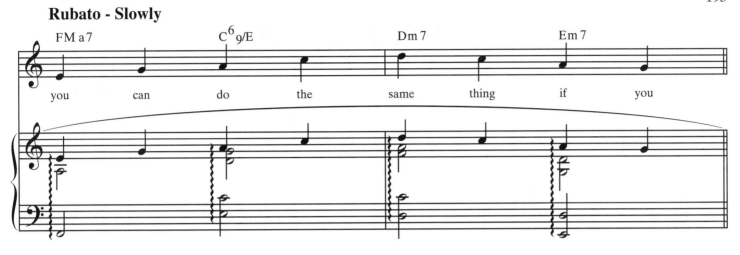

**A Tempo**

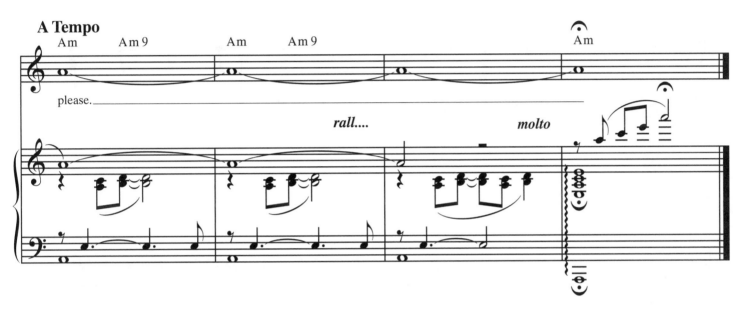

3. The game of life is hard to play.
   I'm going to lose it anyway.
   The losing card I'll someday lay,
   so this is all I have to say.
     That: (chorus)

4. The only way to win, is cheat
   and lay it down before I'm beat,
   and to another give a seat
   for that's the only painless feat.
     'Cause (chorus)

5. The sword of time will pierce our skins.
   It doesn't hurt when it begins,
   but as it works its way on in,
   the pain grows stronger, watch it grin.
     For: (chorus)

6. A brave man once requested me
   to answer questions that are key.
   Is it to be or not to be?
   And I replied; "Oh, why ask me?"
     'Cause (chorus)

*(from Walt Disney's "MARY POPPINS")*

# A SPOONFUL OF SUGAR

Words and Music by
RICHARD M. SHERMAN and
ROBERT B. SHERMAN

In ev - 'ry job that must be done there is an
feath - er - ing his nest has ver - y

el - e - ment of fun; You find the fun and
lit - tle time to rest While gath - er - ing his

snap the job's a game; And ev - 'ry task you un - der-
bits of twine and twig. Though quite in - tent in his pur -

A Spoonful of Sugar - 3 - 1

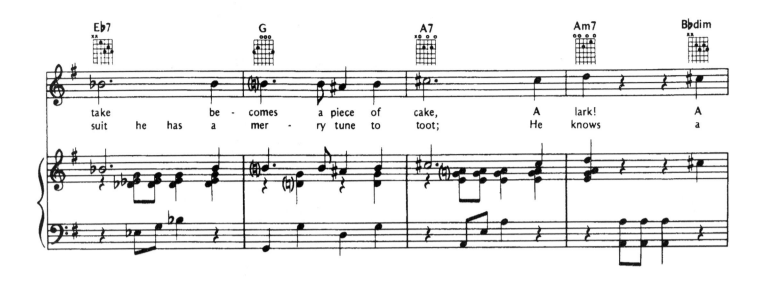

take be - comes a piece of cake, A lark! A
suit he has a mer - ry tune to toot; He knows

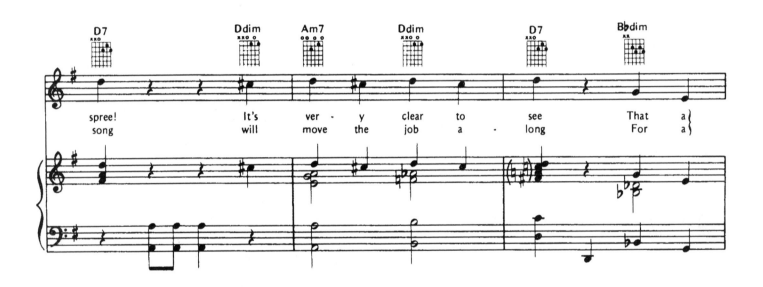

spree! It's ver - y clear to see That a
song will move the job a - long For a

spoon - ful of su - gar helps the med - i - cine go

196

A Spoonful of Sugar - 3 - 3

# STREETS OF PHILADELPHIA

Words and Music by
BRUCE SPRINGSTEEN

Streets of Philadelphia - 3 - 1

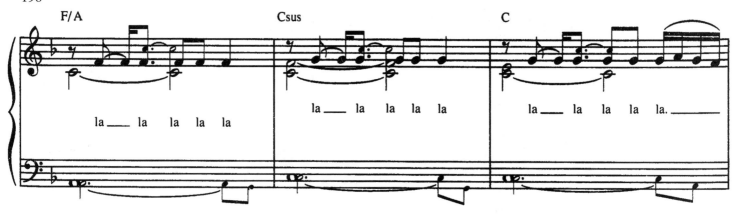

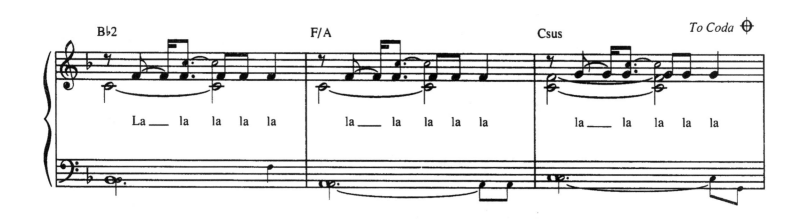

And my clothes don't fit me no more; ___ I walked a thou-sand miles ___ just to ___

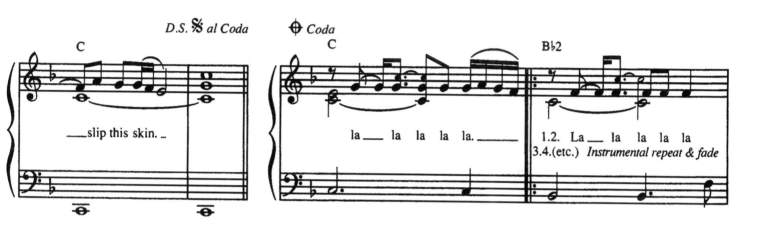

*D.S. %* al Coda   ⊕ *Coda*

___slip this skin. _

la ___ la la la la. _____   1.2. La ___ la la la la

3.4.(etc.) *Instrumental repeat & fade*

*Repeat ad lib. and fade*

la ___ la la la la   la ___ la la la la   la ___ la la la la. _____

*Verse 2:*
I walked the avenue till my legs felt like stone.
I heard the voices of friends vanished and gone.
At night I could hear the blood in my veins
Just as black and whispering as the rain
On the streets of Philadelphia.
*(To Chorus:)*

*Verse 3:*
The night has fallen. I'm lyin' awake.
I can feel myself fading away.
So, receive me, brother, with your faithless kiss,
Or will we leave each other alone like this
On the streets of Philadelphia?
*(To Chorus:)*

# STAR WARS

(Main Title)

(From *Star Wars*®: Episode III *Revenge of the Sith*)

Music by
**JOHN WILLIAMS**

**Majestically, steady march** (♩ = 108)

Star Wars - 4 - 1

# SUPERMAN RETURNS
## (Suite)

By JOHN OTTMAN
*Arranged by DAMON INTRABARTOLO*

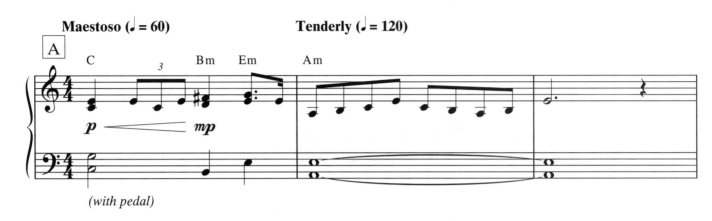

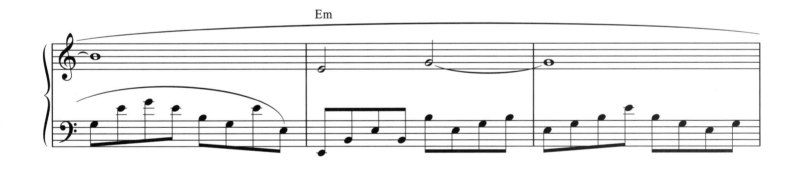

Superman Returns - 7 - 1

206

210

Superman Returns - 7 - 7

# SYRIANA THEME

By ALEXANDRE DESPLAT

Adagio ♩ = 63

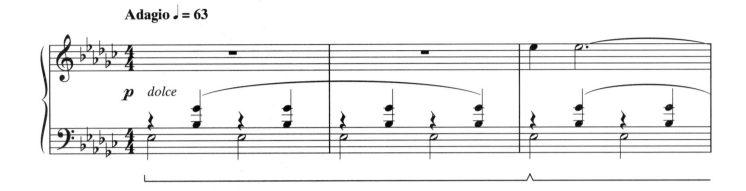

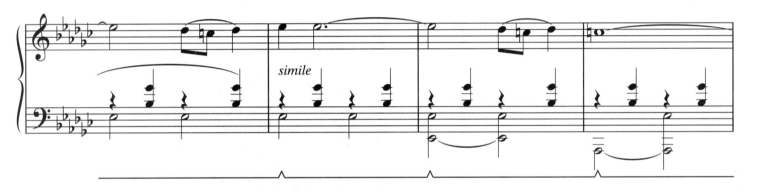

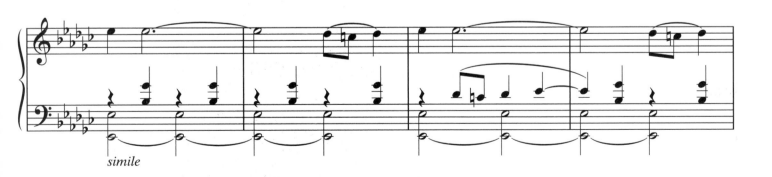

Syriana Theme - 3 - 1

# THAT'S WHAT FRIENDS ARE FOR

Words and Music by
CAROLE BAYER SAGER
and BURT BACHARACH

That's What Friends Are For - 3 - 1

216

That's What Friends Are For - 3 - 3

# THEME FROM A SUMMER PLACE

Words by
MACK DISCANT

Music by
MAX STEINER

218

*(from Walt Disney's "THE LITTLE MERMAID")*

# UNDER THE SEA

Words by
HOWARD ASHMAN

Music by
ALAN MENKEN

Under the Sea - 10 - 1

Bb · Eb · F

Dar - lin' it's   bet - ter   down __ where it's   wet - ter. Take __ it from
No - bod - y   beat us,   fry __ us and   eat us   in __ fri - ca -

Bb · Bb7 · Eb

me.   Up __ on   the shore they   work __ all day.
see.   We __ what   the land folks   loves __ to cook.

F · Gm · C7

Out __ in   the sun they   slave __ a - way.   While __ we de -
Un - der   the sea we   off __ the hook.   We __ got no

Eb · F7 · Bb

vo - tin' full - time to   float - in' un - der the   sea.
trou - bles life __ is the   bub - bles un - der the

224

guine it's mu - sic to me. What __ do they got, a lot __ of sand. We __ got a hot crus - ta - ce - an band. Each __ lit - tle clam here know __ how to jam __ here un - der the sea. Each lit - tle slug here cut - tin' a

# UP WHERE WE BELONG

Words by
WILL JENNINGS

Music by
JACK NITZSCHE and BUFFY SAINTE-MARIE

Up Where We Belong - 4 - 1

232

*Verse 2:*
Some hang on to "used-to-be",
Live their lives looking behind.
All we have is here and now;
All our life, out there to find.
The road is long.
There are mountains in our way,
But we climb them a step every day.

*From Warner Bros. Pictures' CORPSE BRIDE*

# VICTOR'S PIANO SOLO

Music by
DANNY ELFMAN

Victor's Piano Solo - 2 - 1

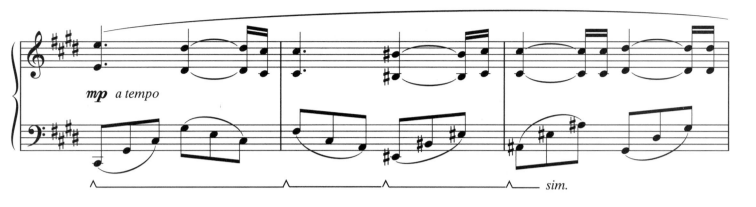

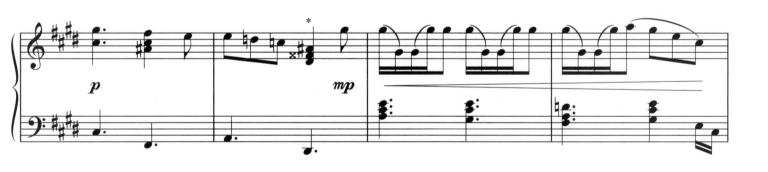

(cluster chords)

*F𝄪 = G♮

# WAY BACK INTO LOVE

from "Music and Lyrics"

Words and Music by
ADAM SCHLESINGER

238

Verses 3 & 4:

F: 3. I've been watch-ing, but the stars re-fuse___ to___ shine.___
M: 4. I've been look-ing for some-one to shed___ some___ light,

___ I've been search-ing, but I just don't see___ the signs.___ I know that it's out

not some-bod-y just to get me through___ the night.___ I could use some di-rec-

___ there. There's got-ta be some-thing for my___ soul, some-where.___

tion, and I'm o-pen to your___

___ sug-ges-tions. All I wan-na do is find___ a way

Chorus:

Both:

Way Back Into Love - 7 - 3

# WHO'S THAT GIRL?

Words and Music by
MADONNA CICCONE
and PAT LEONARD

Who's That Girl? - 5 - 5

# WONKA'S WELCOME SONG

Music by DANNY ELFMAN
Lyrics by JOHN AUGUST and DANNY ELFMAN

Wonka's Welcome Song - 4 - 1

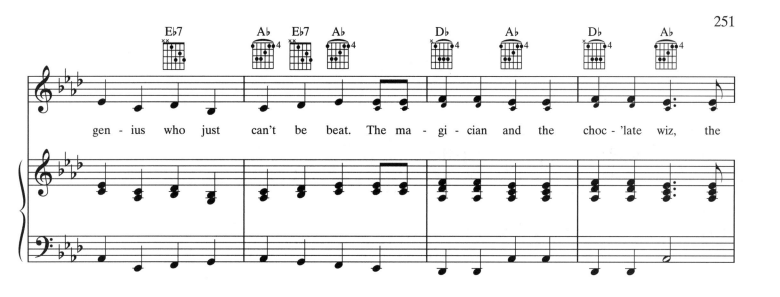

gen - ius who just can't be beat. The ma - gi - cian and the choc - 'late wiz, the

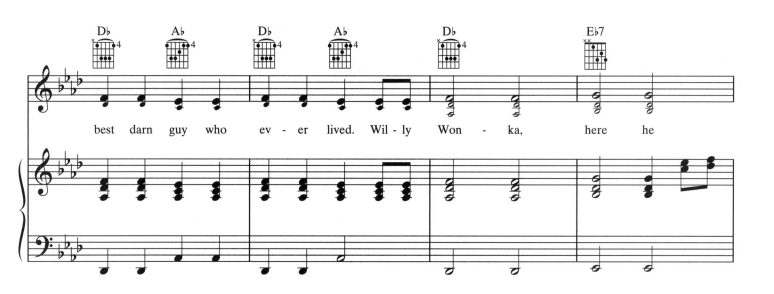

best darn guy who ev - er lived. Wil - ly Won - ka, here he

is!

*(from Walt Disney's "CINDERELLA")*

# THE WORK SONG

Words and Music by
MACK DAVID, AL HOFFMAN
and JERRY LIVINGSTON

The Work Song - 2 - 1

cel - lar, you can do them both to - geth - er, Cin - der - el - la."

Cin - der -

How love - ly it would be⎯⎯
live my fan - ta - sy. ⎯⎯

cresc.    decresc.

⎯ if I could
⎯ But in the mid - dle of my dream - ing⎯⎯ they're

cresc.

scream - ing⎯⎯ at me⎯⎯ Cin - der - el - la."

The Work Song - 2 - 2

*From Warner Bros. Pictures' HARRY POTTER AND THE PRISONER OF AZKABAN*

# A WINDOW TO THE PAST

Music by
**JOHN WILLIAMS**

**Slowly and tenderly** (♩. = 54)

A Window to the Past - 3 - 1